WHAT
Is
REPENTANCE?

The Crucial Questions Series
By R.C. Sproul

WHO *IS* JESUS?

CAN I TRUST *the* BIBLE?

DOES *Prayer* CHANGE THINGS?

CAN I *Know* GOD'S WILL?

HOW SHOULD I *Live* IN THIS WORLD?

WHAT DOES IT MEAN *to Be* BORN AGAIN?

CAN I BE SURE *I'm* SAVED?

WHAT *IS* FAITH?

WHAT CAN I *Do with* MY GUILT?

WHAT *IS the* TRINITY?

WHAT *IS* BAPTISM?

CAN I HAVE *Joy in* MY LIFE?

WHO IS *the* HOLY SPIRIT?

DOES GOD *Control* EVERYTHING?

How Can I Develop a CHRISTIAN CONSCIENCE?

WHAT *IS the* LORD'S SUPPER?

WHAT IS *the* CHURCH?

WHAT *IS* REPENTANCE?

WHAT IS *the Relationship between* CHURCH *and* STATE?

ARE THESE *the* LAST DAYS?

CRUCIAL
QUESTIONS
No. | 18

WHAT
Is
REPENTANCE?

R.C. SPROUL

IR *Reformation Trust*   A DIVISION OF LIGONIER MINISTRIES, ORLANDO, FL

What Is Repentance?

© 2014 by R.C. Sproul

Published by Reformation Trust Publishing
A division of Ligonier Ministries
421 Ligonier Court, Sanford, FL 32771
Ligonier.org   ReformationTrust.com

Printed in North Mankato, MN
Corporate Graphics
June 2016
First edition, fourth printing

Cover design: Gearbox Studios
Interior design and typeset: Katherine Lloyd, The DESK

All Scripture quotations are from *The Holy Bible, English Standard Version*,
copyright © 2001 by Crossway Bibles, a division of Good News Publishers. Used
by permission. All rights reserved.

Library of Congress Cataloging-in-Publication Data

Sproul, R. C. (Robert Charles), 1939-
  What is repentance? / by R.C. Sproul. -- First edition.
     pages cm. -- (Crucial questions series ; No. 18)
  Includes bibliographical references.
  ISBN 978-1-56769-372-0 -- ISBN 1-56769-372-5
1. Repentance--Christianity. I. Title.
  BT800.S67 2014
  234'.5--dc23

                                          2014006855

Contents

One—WHAT IS REPENTANCE? 1

Two—A PICTURE OF REPENTANCE 9

Three—A MODEL OF REPENTANCE 19

Four—REGENERATION AND REPENTANCE 29

Chapter One

WHAT IS
REPENTANCE?

Have you ever been asked what you would do differently if you had your life to live over again? It amazes me when people respond that they wouldn't do anything differently. I simply can't imagine someone not having anything they'd want to change. Don't we all have regrets? Certainly, as Christians who understand our sin, we would relish the chance to relive some of our past. Perhaps we have words we'd love to take back or painful scenes we'd like to rewrite.

These desires hint at our need for repentance.

It is vitally important that we understand the biblical concept of repentance. It is central, not only to the New Testament, but to all of Scripture. The gospel of Mark begins with the appearance of John the Baptist, who comes out of the wilderness announcing the approach of the kingdom of God. His message to the people of Israel was very simple: he called them to repentance. Just a short time after this, Jesus began His public ministry, preaching the exact same message: "Now after John was arrested, Jesus came into Galilee, proclaiming the gospel of God, and saying, 'The time is fulfilled, and the kingdom of God is at hand; repent and believe in the gospel'" (Mark 1:14–15).

This theme recurs throughout the New Testament. When people listened to Christ or to the preaching of the Apostles, they would often respond by asking, "What should we do?" The answers assumed a similar form— "Believe in Christ," "Believe and be baptized," or "Repent and be baptized." Since this concept of repentance is so central to the Apostolic preaching, it's extremely important that we fully understand it.

The word *repentance* comes from a Greek word *metanoia*. The prefix *meta* can mean "with," "beside," or "after."

An English derivative is *metaphysics*. The study of physics is the study of those elements of nature that are visible, perceivable, and physical. Metaphysics is an attempt to reach beyond the realm of the physical world to the transcendent realm. The root *noia* is the verb form of the noun that we find frequently in the Bible as *nous*. This is simply the Greek word for "mind." In its simplest form, the term *metanoia* has to do with "the mind afterward," or, as we might say, "an afterthought." In the Greek language, it came to mean "a significant changing of one's mind."

So, in the most rudimentary sense, the concept of repentance in the Bible means "to change one's mind." However, we will soon see that this is not just a matter of intellectual judgment, such as changing our approach after trying to solve a problem. Generally speaking, *metanoia* has to do with the changing of one's mind with respect to one's behavior. It contains the idea of *ruing*. To rue something means to regret a particular action. It carries with it not only an intellectual assessment but also an emotional or visceral response. The feeling most often associated with repentance in Scripture is that of remorse, regret, and a sense of sorrow for having acted in a particular way. Thus, repentance involves sorrow for a previous form of behavior.

The concept of repentance is deeply rooted in the experience of Old Testament Israel. When scholars examine the Old Testament understanding of repentance, they often make a distinction between two kinds of repentance. The first is cultic or ritualistic repentance and the second is prophetic repentance.

First, let's consider cultic or ritualistic repentance. In our day, the word *cultic* can be very misleading. When we use the term *cult*, we think of fringe groups of people led by false teachers. But the term *cultic*, used in the true theological sense, refers not to aberrant groups but to the behavioral patterns or the religious life of a given community. Israel's *cultus* in the Old Testament was its communal practice of religious observances. God is the One who instituted the cultus of Israel. By His law, He defined not only how the people were to behave morally, but also how they were to behave religiously. For example, there were instructions for how to pray, how to offer sacrifices, and how to carry out the ministrations of temple worship. These were all part of the cultic practices of Israel.

Similarly, the religious structure of Old Testament life included many practices aimed at facilitating repentance. God's wrath would burn against His people for their faithless disobedience, and as a result, they would follow His instructions on how to remove His wrath from them. God would forgive their sins, and peace with Him would be restored in the community. Repentance rituals in the Old Testament often included a call for fasting during a solemn assembly. When the Israelites were in the wilderness, they were first brought before the tabernacle and then later to the temple. The prophet would announce God's judgment and call for a general fast. To turn God's wrath away, everyone would go without food for a particular period of time as a national sign of repentance.

God's people, Israel, were also instructed to wear certain types of clothing that would function as an outward symbol of an inner repentant heart. For example, we read of people wearing "sackcloth and ashes." Many would wear coarse, uncomfortable cloth as a type of a punitive measure, inflicting discomfort as a mark of repentance. Some might also take ashes and spread them on their clothes or across their foreheads. This ritualistic process was a sign of self-abasement. For example, after God spoke to Job from the whirlwind, Job said, "Therefore I despise myself, and repent in dust and ashes" (Job 42:6).

Along with the change of clothes, there was a particular

type of song that was sung. It was a lament, a song that expressed grief. Sometimes, the lament would be used when someone died or a catastrophe took place. In the Old Testament, the book of Jeremiah is followed by a shorter book called Lamentations, also written by Jeremiah. In this book, Jeremiah laments God's wrath having been poured out upon His impenitent people in the destruction of Jerusalem. This is a prime example of this kind of sorrow for sin. True penitence was to be expressed with the lament, a song of grief, and accompanied by loud cries and wailing.

In addition, specific prayers of repentance were part of the religious system of Israel. The book of Psalms, as a type of hymnal for God's people, contains prayers and poetry put to music and sung as part of the liturgy of the Israelite community. It is made up of different genres: psalms of lament, psalms of thanksgiving, and royal psalms, among others. There are psalms celebrating the goodness of God's law, but also psalms called penitential psalms, which were a kind of lament. Penitential psalms include an acknowledgement of sin against God, a resolution to turn away from the evil behavior, and a humble plea that God would restore the people to a state of grace. The most famous of the penitential psalms is Psalm 51. In this Psalm, David records his emotional confession of sin after being confronted by Nathan the prophet for his sins against Uriah and Bathsheba.

A final feature of this ritualistic life were specific days of repentance. These days were set apart not only for feasts, celebrations, and remembrances of the past, but also for penitence. They were set times for corporate acknowledgement and sorrow for sin, and they formed a part of the cultic life of Israel.

The cultic practices and rituals of the Old Testament allowed the people of Israel to express, verbalize, and demonstrate their sorrow for sin. But how do we do this today? How do we show a broken heart for having offended God? How do we demonstrate this in the life of the church?

In the Roman Catholic Church, a whole system of penance is tied into the sacraments of the church, but Protestants seem to have lost their way in terms of having a prescribed method of showing repentance. Among the few practices that exist to facilitate repentance is the occasional prayer on Sunday morning in which the congregation confesses its sin corporately and receives assurance of pardon from the minister.

With particular forms of repentance comes the danger

of mere externalism; as we will see, primary importance should be given to the heart. However, we often lack the ability to demonstrate our repentance. Here, we, like the people of the Old Testament, might find it helpful to have more structured ways to demonstrate this change of heart.

Chapter Two

A Picture of Repentance

As a small boy, I was part of the children's choir at church. I didn't participate because of religious devotion or zeal, but because my parents forced me to do so. Choir was embarrassing, since I had to dress up in a cassock and white surplice with a large starched white collar and black bow. Other boys would call me "Little Lord Fauntleroy."

We sang once every two months as part of the worship service, but the highlight for the boys' choir was when we sang the anthem "Seek Ye the Lord." On this particular piece, the lead soloist, a magnificent tenor from the adult choir, assisted us. I wasn't a Christian then, but this song was so magnificently sung that the words stuck with me. The power of God's Word was woven all through this song, and as it was sung, the Word would percolate in my soul and in my mind.

This was many decades ago, but I can still see Dick Dodds standing in the choir loft, singing, "Seek ye the Lord while He may be found. Call ye upon Him while He is near. Let the wicked forsake his thoughts and the unrighteous man his way. For He will have mercy. He will have mercy. He will have mercy and abundantly pardon." These words were taken right from the words of the prophets (in this case, Isaiah 55), who were profoundly concerned about true repentance and its place in the life of God's people.

We've already considered the Jewish Old Testament rituals, which included the cultic practices of fasting, the day of repentance, the changing of clothes, and songs of lament. Over time, these practices and rituals degenerated into mere externalism for many people. Worshipers simply went through the motions of repentance while lacking real sincerity. During the eighth and seventh centuries BC, great prophets such as Amos, Jeremiah, Isaiah, and Hosea came to the people to remind them that God demands genuine, godly sorrow that comes from the heart. The bottom line was this: the people were called to rend their hearts, not their garments. When the prophets exhorted the people in this way, they weren't opposing the practice of the rending of garments, but were saying that it's not enough to tear your clothes as a sign of repentance; the heart must be torn as well. When we realize that we have offended God, we must feel this rupture of our soul.

To get a better handle on this prophetic approach to repentance, let's consider the book of Joel. This book focuses on the relationship between the rituals of repentance and the reality that those rituals are designed to symbolize. In the first chapter, we read of Joel's calling for a solemn assembly so that the people can hear an announcement from God.

> The word of the Lord that came to Joel, the son of Pethuel:
>
> Hear this, you elders; give ear, all inhabitants of the land! Has such a thing happened in your days, or in the days of your fathers? Tell your children

of it, and let your children tell their children, and their children to another generation.

What the cutting locust left, the swarming locust has eaten. What the swarming locust left, the hopping locust has eaten, and what the hopping locust left, the destroying locust has eaten. (Joel 1:1–4)

A severe judgment had fallen on God's people. The land had been destroyed by drought and the invasion of insects consuming the people's crops. All of this is perceived by the prophet as the hand of God's judgment on the people for their sin. Therefore, the people are called to turn, to change their mind, to repent.

Joel says, "Awake, you drunkards, and weep, and wail, all you drinkers of wine, because of the sweet wine, for it is cut off from your mouth" (v. 5). Even the crops of the vineyards had been destroyed, and those who were lying around in a drunken stupor were called to wake up and see that even the pleasure that they received from the fruit of the vine had dried up. Joel is announcing that the day of repentance has come.

He continues, "Lament like a virgin wearing sackcloth

for the bridegroom of her youth" (v. 8). For most women, the selection of a wedding dress is of utmost importance. The bride will be the center of attention as she walks down the aisle to be lawfully wed to her awaiting fiancé. Attendees "ooh" and "ahh" as they see the woman dressed in the finest gown she will ever wear. Here, the prophet Joel says Israel is like a bride who is adorned not in a beautiful gown, but in sackcloth. Imagine going to a wedding where the bride enters wearing a worn-out, ugly burlap bag. This is the image Joel uses to show how repentance is supposed to be demonstrated. It is a stark picture of mourning in the place of rejoicing.

Joel writes, "The priests mourn, the ministers of the LORD. The fields are destroyed, the ground mourns, because the grain is destroyed, the wine dries up, the oil languishes" (vv. 9b–10). In the economy of ancient Israel, olive oil was quite important. The prophet is saying, "The whole national economy of Israel is now bankrupt. Everything has dried up. Be ashamed, you farmers. Wail, you vine dressers. Wail for the wheat and the barley because the harvest in the field has perished and joy has withered away."

In verse 13, we see again the instructions for showing repentance. "Put on sackcloth and lament, O priests; wail,

O ministers of the altar. Go in, pass the night in sackcloth, O ministers of my God! Because grain offering and drink offering are withheld from the house of your God" (v. 13). Notice that the weightiest call for penance in this time of national calamity is given to the priests. They were the ones who held the burden of the national guilt. The prophets of Israel functioned as the nation's conscience, and the prophets' task of calling the priests to repentance was particularly difficult. As the priests became corrupt, true godliness was concealed from the people. Instead of training the people in godliness, the false prophets and the corrupt priests attempted to please the people rather than ministering to them. Instead of exhorting the people, they complimented them. Instead of calling the people to repentance when they sinned, the priests colluded with the people, making them feel good rather than risking offending them. It was a feel-good type of religion. But the prophet comes with the Word of God and says to the ministers, "Wail, cry, and lie down in sackcloth and ashes."

The next verse reads, "Consecrate a fast; call a solemn assembly. Gather the elders and all the inhabitants of the land to the house of the LORD your God, and cry out to the LORD" (v. 14). All of these are elements of the cultic rituals of repentance in the Old Testament. Later, we read, "'Yet even now,' declares the LORD, 'return to me with all your heart, with fasting, with weeping, and with mourning; and rend your hearts and not your garments'" (2:12–13a).

The central concept of repentance in the Old Testament can be captured in one word: *conversion*. This word is frequently heard in the jargon that Christians use today and is the focal point of the prophetic call to repentance. No one is born biologically as a Christian. In order for one to become a Christian, something has to happen by which that person is radically changed. This is linked to the biblical concept of *metanoia*, that change of mind that is not merely an intellectual adjustment of a concept but the turning around of one's entire life. To the prophet, repentance is not merely a religious ritual, but is integral to conversion of the soul. It means a change of one's entire being.

In everyone's life there is a turning point, a crucial moment that defines our existence. It might be meeting a certain person, getting a particular job, or experiencing a particular disaster. For the nation of Israel, that point was its founding by God. God gave the people their identity as His chosen people, entered into a covenant with them, and gave them certain precepts that they were to follow. The people vowed that they would follow after God, that they would obey His commandments, and that they would love Him with all of their hearts. But time after time, the nation turned away, and so the prophets came to the nation and said, "You have to turn around and return to the Lord."

Before sin entered the world, there was a time when the whole race was incorporated in our federal head, Adam, who represented us before God and enjoyed obedience before God and perfect fellowship with Him. Milton wrote about this in his epic work *Paradise Lost*. We lost paradise when we turned away from God and each person turned to his own way. So today, when we call people to conversion, it's still appropriate to think of it in terms of "going home"—back to where we were originally, in the presence of God, in fellowship with God, and in submission to God. The call to repentance is a call to return, a call to go back home.

The most important turning point in my life was my conversion; there's no other event in my life that had such a radical impact on everything that followed. My whole life was changed and turned upside down. No, I wasn't made perfect or rid of sin overnight. But in this *metanoia*, this changing of the mind, the direction of my life was radically altered. Before *metanoia*, before the repentance of conversion, one's life is moving away from God. The longer we live in impenitence, and the longer we remain in an unconverted state, the farther we move away from God. Conversion doesn't mean we instantly jump from sin to perfection, but that our lives are fundamentally turned around. From the moment of our conversion, our lives are moving in a different direction, back toward God.

Think of the most crucial turning points in your life. What were those moments, the decisions, or the events that turned you away from God? What were those moments in your life that changed you for the better? Now ask yourself: Are you a converted person? Where are you headed? What direction are you moving? Does your life need to turn?

Chapter Three

A MODEL OF REPENTANCE

In Shakespeare's *Macbeth*, there is a powerful metaphor for repentance. Lady Macbeth, the ambitious and cunning wife of the play's protagonist, is wracked with guilt over her part in the murder of King Duncan. One night, as she sleepwalks and hallucinates, she recalls her crimes. In anguish, she attempts to wash the blood from her hands. However, there is no soap strong enough to remove the stain of her guilt, and she cries, "Out, damned spot!"

This image of being made clean is at the heart of the biblical concept of repentance. We may be tempted to think of repentance merely in terms of forgiveness, but it is also about cleansing. We are corrupt, and we must be made clean. We may also be tempted to think of repentance as an optional add-on to faith. Justification, after all, is by faith *alone*. But justification does not exclude repentance. Repentance is not a tangential concept in the Bible; rather, it is central in conversion and justification.

Our guide in exploring these themes will be Psalm 51. One of the penitential psalms, this psalm was written by David after he was confronted by the prophet Nathan. Nathan declared that David had grievously sinned against God in the taking of Bathsheba to be his wife and in the murder of her husband, Uriah.

It's important to see the anguish and heartfelt remorse expressed by David, but we must also understand that repentance of the heart is the work of God the Holy Spirit. David is repentant because of the influence of the Holy Spirit upon him. Not only that, but as he writes this prayer, he is writing it under the inspiration of the Holy Spirit. The Holy Spirit demonstrates in Psalm 51 how He produces repentance in our hearts. Keep this in mind as we look at the psalm.

Psalm 51 begins, "Have mercy on me, O God, according to your steadfast love; according to your abundant mercy blot out my transgressions" (v. 1). Here we see an element that is fundamental to repentance. Usually, when a person becomes aware of his sin and turns from it, he casts himself on the mercy of God. The first fruit of authentic repentance is the recognition of our profound need for mercy. David does not ask God for justice. He knows that if God were to deal with him according to justice, he would be immediately destroyed. As a result, David begins his confession with a plea for mercy.

When David pleads with God to blot out his transgressions, he's asking God to remove the stain from his soul, to cover his unrighteousness, and to cleanse him from the sin that is now a permanent part of his life. So he says, "Wash me thoroughly from my iniquity, and cleanse me from my sin!" (v. 2).

The ideas of forgiveness and cleansing are related, but they are not the same thing. In the New Testament, the Apostle John writes, "If we confess our sins, he is faithful and just to forgive us our sins and to cleanse us from all unrighteousness" (1 John 1:9). In a spirit of repentance, we go before God and confess our sins, asking not only for the pardon, but also for the strength to refrain from doing that sin anymore. As David does in this psalm, we ask that our inclination to wickedness be eliminated.

David continues, "For I know my transgressions, and my sin is ever before me" (Ps. 51:3). This isn't simply a casual acknowledgement of guilt. He is a haunted man; he says, "I know I am guilty." There's no attempt to minimize his guilt. There's no attempt at self-justification. We, however, are often masters of rationalization and are quick to excuse ourselves by giving all kinds of reasons for our sinful behavior. But in this text, by the power of the Holy Spirit, David is brought to the point where he is honest before God. He admits his guilt, realizing that his sin is ever present. He can't get rid of it, and this haunts him.

Then he cries out, "Against you, you only, have I sinned and done what is evil in your sight" (v. 4a). In one sense, David is using hyperbole here. He has sinned horribly against Uriah, Uriah's family and friends, Bathsheba, and the whole nation of God's people. But David understands that sin ultimately is an offense against God, because God is the only perfect being in the universe. As God is the judge of heaven and earth, all sin is defined in terms of the transgression of God's law and is an offense against His holiness. David knows this and acknowledges it. He's not minimizing the reality of his sin against human beings, but he recognizes the ultimacy of his sin against God.

He then makes a statement that is often overlooked. It's found in the second part of verse 4 and is one of the most powerful expressions of true repentance that we find in the Scriptures: "so that you may be justified in your words and blameless in your judgment" (v. 4b). David is essentially saying, "O God, You have every right to judge me, and it is clear that I deserve nothing more than Your judgment and Your wrath." David acknowledges that God is blameless and has every right to judge him. There is no bargaining or negotiating with God.

"Behold, I was brought forth in iniquity, and in sin did my mother conceive me. Behold, you delight in truth in the inward being, and you teach me wisdom in the secret heart" (vv. 5–6). Not only does God wants the truth from us, He wants it from deep within us. David acknowledges that he has failed to do what God has commanded, and that his obedience is often mere external ceremony rather than acts that flow out of the center of his being.

Then David cries out again for cleansing: "Purge me with hyssop, and I shall be clean; wash me, and I shall be whiter than snow" (v. 7). We can hear the utter help-lessness in David's voice. David doesn't say, "God, wait a minute. Before I continue this dialogue in prayer, I have to clean my hands. I have to get washed." David knows that he's incapable of removing the stain of his guilt from himself. He cannot make up for it. We must join David in acknowledging that we cannot atone for our own sins.

Through the prophet Isaiah, God later gave this prom-ise, "Come now, let us reason together, says the LORD: though your sins are like scarlet, they shall be as white as snow; though they are red like crimson, they shall become like wool" (Isa. 1:18). God is pleased to clean us up when He finds us in the dirt.

David then says, "Let me hear joy and gladness" (Ps. 51:8a). Repentance is a painful thing. Who enjoys going through the confession of sin and the acknowledgement of guilt? Guilt is the most powerful destroyer of joy there is. While David is not very happy at this moment, he asks God to restore his soul and make him feel joy and gladness again. He makes this point when he says, "Let the bones that you have broken rejoice" (v. 8b). Isn't that an interesting phrase? He says, "God, You've crushed me. My bones are broken; it wasn't Satan or Nathan that broke my bones, but you broke my bones when you convicted me of my guilt. So, I stand before you as a broken man, and the only way I can go on is if You heal me and return joy and gladness to me."

Next he says, "Hide your face from my sins, and blot out all my iniquities. Create in me a clean heart, O God, and renew a right spirit within me" (v. 9–10). The only way to have a clean heart is by a work of divine re-creation. I am incapable of creating that in myself. Only God can create a clean heart, and He *does* create clean hearts by blotting out our sin.

David then cries, "Cast me not away from your presence, and take not your Holy Spirit from me" (v. 11). David realizes that this is the worst thing that could happen to any sinner. He knows that God will, in fact, cast us out of His presence if we persist in impenitence. Jesus warns that those who reject Him will be cut off from God forever. But the prayer of repentance is a refuge for the believer. It is the godly response of one who knows that he is in sin. This type of response should mark the lives of all those who are converted.

David continues, "Restore to me the joy of your salvation, and uphold me with a willing spirit. Then I will teach transgressors your ways, and sinners will return to you" (vv.

12–13). We often hear that people don't like to be in the presence of Christians because Christians manifest a smug, self-righteous attitude or a goody-two-shoes, holier-than-thou attitude. But this should not be the case. Christians have nothing to be smug about; we are not righteous people trying to correct the unrighteous. As one preacher said, "Evangelism is just one beggar telling another beggar where to find bread." The chief difference between the believer and the unbeliever is forgiveness. The only thing that qualifies a person to be a minister in the name of Christ is that that person has experienced forgiveness and wants to tell of it to others.

"O Lord, open my lips, and my mouth will declare your praise. For you will not delight in sacrifice, or I would give it; you will not be pleased with a burnt offering. The sacrifices of God are a broken spirit; a broken and contrite heart, O God, you will not despise" (vv. 15–17). Here's where we find the heart and soul of prophetic repentance as seen in the last chapter. The true nature of godly repentance is found in the phrase "a broken and contrite heart, O God, you will not despise." David is saying that if he could atone for his own sins, he would; but as it is, his only hope is that God would accept him according to His mercy.

The Bible tells us explicitly and shows us implicitly that God resists the proud and gives grace to the humble. David knows this to be true. As broken as he is, he knows God and how God relates to penitent people. He understands that God never hates or despises a broken and contrite heart. This is what God desires from us. This is what Jesus had in mind in the Beatitudes when He said, "Blessed are those who mourn, for they shall be comforted" (Matt. 5:4). This text is not simply about grieving the loss of a loved one, but also the grief that we experience when convicted by our sin. Jesus assures us that when we grieve over our sin, God by His Holy Spirit will comfort us.

I would recommend that all Christians memorize Psalm 51. It is a perfect model of godly repentance. Many times in my life, I have come to the Lord and said, "Create in me a clean heart, O God," or, "Blot out my transgressions. Purge me with hyssop. Wash me and make me clean." Many times I've prayed, "O Lord, restore to me the joy of your salvation," and cried out, "Against you, you only have I sinned." When we feel overwhelmed by the reality of our guilt, words fail us as we seek to express ourselves in penitence before God. It truly is a blessing to have the words of Scripture themselves upon our lips on those occasions.

Chapter Four

REGENERATION
AND REPENTANCE

Many centuries ago, Saint Augustine created a bit of controversy with a simple prayer. Augustine prayed, "Grant what Thou dost command, and command what Thou wilt." Augustine's famous theological sparring partner, Pelagius, was not pleased, and reacted quite negatively. He argued that if God commands something, reason would indicate that we are able, without any assistance from God, to do what He commands.

But Augustine recognized what Pelagius refused to admit—that we are fallen creatures, and since the fall, we are morally incapable of doing everything that God commands. The fall infects us all the way down to the level of our abilities. For example, God commands perfect obedience, and who among us is able to give that kind of obedience to God? God commands that we be holy in the same manner in which He is holy, but we are unholy; as fallen creatures we do not have the moral power for holiness within us. The Bible says we are under the power of sin, not just under the judgment of the law. Sin has a vise-like grip on our hearts. This is made plain when we as Christians battle specific sins over and over again.

One of the great themes of the New Testament is that God, in His grace, enables us to do what He commands. His primary command is to repent. This is the message of both John the Baptist and Jesus at the beginning of their ministries. Yet how can we repent if we are completely under the power of sin?

Genuine repentance is something that is worked in us by the Holy Spirit. It is a gracious activity by God. We have seen that conversion and repentance are inseparably linked. If we look carefully at the New Testament concept of faith, which is the supreme requirement for redemption, we learn that godly repentance is an integral part of faith. If a person has faith but not repentance, that person does not have authentic faith. That person does not possess the necessary ingredients for redemption; conversion is a result of faith *and* repentance.

The New Testament tells us that faith is a gift of God. Faith is not something produced by our own power, but it is wrought by the Holy Spirit. This is called "rebirth" or "regeneration." If we asked one hundred Christians to answer this question, "Which comes first, regeneration or repentance?" I imagine that ninety out of a hundred would say repentance comes first. However, it doesn't make sense that people who are dead in their sins and trespasses would incline themselves naturally to repentance. The New Testament teaches that God the Holy Spirit first quickens our souls, making us alive spiritually, and the fruit of this work is godly repentance and faith.

Consider Ephesians 2:1–2a: "And you were dead in the trespasses and sins in which you once walked." Paul is addressing believers in Ephesus, and he's reminding them of what God, in His grace, has done for them. Paul insists that if you're a Christian, God has made you alive. When?

When He resuscitated you. He raised you from the dead, not physically, but spiritually. You were dead in your state of sin. Paul is saying, "You used to be unconverted, and God has converted you. You used to be dead. God has resurrected you. God has made you alive to Himself."

Paul writes, "And you were dead in the trespasses and sins in which you once walked, following the course of this world, following the prince of the power of the air, the spirit that is now at work in the sons of disobedience" (vv. 1–2). He's describing the lifestyle of the unconverted and explains that that is where the Ephesians believers used to find themselves.

Most races, like a marathon, have a course that is defined by set boundaries. If you run the race, you have to follow the course. Paul is saying that all of us who are converted used to walk according to a certain course—the course of the world. We were unable to run any other race. This brings to mind Psalm 1:

Blessed is the man who walks not in the counsel of the wicked, nor stands in the way of sinners, nor sits in the seat of scoffers; but his delight is in the law of the Lord, and on his law he meditates day and night.

He is like a tree planted by streams of water that yields its fruit in its season, and its leaf does not wither. In all that he does, he prospers. (Ps. 1:1-4)

The difference between the blessed person and the ungodly person is that the blessed person walks according to the course of heaven and not according to the course of this world. Paul is emphasizing a similar sentiment in Ephesians. There is a marked contrast between the life of the converted person and the life of the unconverted person. The unconverted person is still dead spiritually, walking according to the course of this world.

Before we're converted, we choose to do whatever Satan wants us to do. We're allies in his kingdom, marching to his orders. We walk according to the values and the systems of this world, and we are obedient servants, indeed, slaves, of the prince of the power of the air, or, as Paul puts it, "the spirit that is now at work in the sons of disobedience" (Eph. 2:2b). Paul makes it clear that this was our collective past: "among whom we all once lived in the passions of our flesh, carrying out the desires of the body and the mind, and were by nature children of wrath, like the rest of mankind" (v. 3). Paul is saying that all of us, by nature, are children of wrath. All of us, by nature, are obedient disciples of Satan. No one is born a Christian. In order to become a disciple of Christ, you have to have a *metanoia,* a change of the mind that is reflected in repentance. We have to be raised from spiritual deadness.

However, Paul doesn't leave us in the depths of despair. The next two words, "But God," are two of the most glorious words in the entire Bible. "But God, being rich in mercy, because of the great love with which he loved us, even when we were dead in our trespasses, made us alive together with Christ" (vv. 4–5a). This is crucial. It's not that He made us alive after we inclined ourselves to Him. Paul makes reference to the chronology according to which God spiritually awakens dead people. Christians have been awakened by the rich mercy of God. When? While we were dead in trespasses. Paul is teaching that conversion is a transition from spiritual death to spiritual life. It's a work that only God can do, and He does it for us when we are completely helpless. If you are a converted person, you were converted not because of your own inherent righteousness. You were converted because God converted you.

Paul goes on: "But God, being rich in mercy, because of the great love with which he loved us, even when we were dead in our trespasses, made us alive together with Christ—by grace you have been saved—and raised us up with him and seated us with him in the heavenly places in Christ Jesus, so that in the coming ages he might show the immeasurable riches of his grace in kindness toward us in Christ Jesus. For by grace you have been saved through faith. And this is not your own doing; it is the gift of God" (vv. 4–8). What is the antecedent of the word "this" in the last sentence of this glorious text? In the structure of the text, there's only one thing to which "this" can refer: the entire previous phrase in the text. The "this" refers not just to "grace" or "saved" but also to "faith." By grace have you been saved through faith, and this faith is not something you conjured up all by yourself. Rather, it is a gift of God.

Paul next says that our faith is "not a result of works, so that no one may boast" (v. 9b). We can never boast about conversion, because conversion is all God's work. If there's any question, Paul continues by saying, "For we are his workmanship, created in Christ Jesus for good works"

(v. 10a). We are not re-created by ourselves and by our good works. We are the craftsmanship of Christ. Christ has shaped us and molded us *for* good works. Our good works are the fruit of conversion.

Are you a converted person? The race of life that you are running follows a definite course. Which course is it? Are you running the race of God, or are you following the course of this world? Is your heart's delight to please God? Is there evidence that you are being molded, crafted, and shaped by Christ? Or do you remain cold of heart toward the things of God and estranged from Christ? Are you one of those people who say, "Well, you may find something meaningful in the Christian religion, and Christ may be a crutch for you, but I don't need Christ"? If you're saying that, what you mean is: "I don't want Him. I have no place for Him in my life. I want to craft my own soul and carve my own destiny." These are the signs of an unconverted person. They are the marks of spiritual death.

But there is no greater blessing than to be shaped, molded, and crafted by the gentle working of Christ. That is why Augustine prayed the way he did: "Grant what Thou dost command, and command what Thou wilt." If you know you should repent, but you can't produce feelings of repentance in yourself, pray that God would work repentance in you, because the only one who can produce genuine repentance in your soul is God. God convicts us of sin. God awakens us to our guilt. If God crushes us in godly sorrow, it is an act of sheer grace. It's His act of mercy to bring us to faith and conversion.

About the Author

Dr. R.C. Sproul is the founder and chairman of Ligonier Ministries, an international multimedia ministry based in Sanford, Florida. He also serves as copastor at Saint Andrew's, a Reformed congregation in Sanford, and as chancellor of Reformation Bible College, and his teaching can be heard around the world on the daily radio program *Renewing Your Mind*.

During his distinguished academic career, Dr. Sproul helped train men for the ministry as a professor at several theological seminaries.

He is the author of more than ninety books, including *The Holiness of God*, *Chosen by God*, *The Invisible Hand*, *Faith Alone*, *Everyone's a Theologian*, *Truths We Confess*, *The Truth of the Cross*, and *The Prayer of the Lord*. He also served as general editor of *The Reformation Study Bible* and has written several children's books, including *The Donkey Who Carried a King*.

Dr. Sproul and his wife, Vesta, make their home in Sanford, Florida.

Further your Bible study with *Tabletalk* magazine, another learning tool from R.C. Sproul.

....

TABLETALK MAGAZINE FEATURES:

• A Bible study for each day—bringing the best in biblical scholarship together with down-to-earth writing, *Tabletalk* helps you understand the Bible and apply it to daily living.

• Trusted theological resource—*Tabletalk* avoids trends, shallow doctrine and popular movements to present biblical truth simply and clearly.

• Thought-provoking topics—each issue contains challenging, stimulating articles on a wide variety of topics related to theology and Christian living.

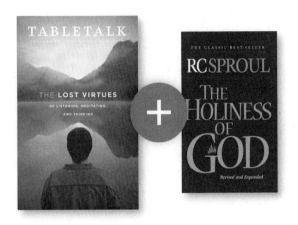

Sign up for a free 3-month trial of *Tabletalk* magazine and we will send you R.C. Sproul's *The Holiness of God*